Rhyme and Shine

Yoga Sun Salutation for Kids

Karen Thygerson

Summary: The classic Yoga sequence of Sun Salutation is presented in fun, easy-to-understand verse for children and their caregivers.

Beau Fait Media

Rhyme and Shine: Yoga Sun Salutation for Kids
Published by Beau Fait Media
©2013 Karen Thygerson
all rights reserved
978-0615858067
0615858066
www.rhymeandshineyoga.com

Peace:
It does not mean to be in
a place where there is no
noise, trouble, or hard work.
It means to be in the midst
of those things and still
be calm in your heart.

—unknown

For Lyla and Jonah, my little yogis. You've been my truest Yoga teachers. Thank you for your Divine spark. Namaste.

Let's find your light inside today
with Sun Salutation,
the Yoga way.

Do the right side,
step by step.
Then repeat it on the left.

Bodies get warm
and minds grow quiet
with every pose you do.
Let's try it!

Stand up tall,
chest out—look proud.
Reach your head
up toward a cloud.

This is **mountain**,
strong and sure,
rooted in the earth so pure.

Breathe in, reach up,
breathe out, dive down.
In forward bend
reach toward the ground.

Still keep your legs
straight and strong.
Your neck is loose and
arms are long.

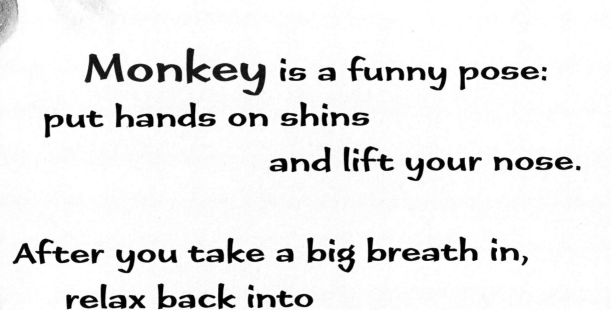

Monkey is a funny pose:
put hands on shins

and lift your nose.

After you take a big breath in,
relax back into

forward bend.

In **lunge**, your right foot
reaches back.
Put both hands down
to stay on track.

Back leg is straight, front knee
over
toes.

This is a very
powerful pose!

To make a **plank**,
        put both feet back.
    Keep breathing!
            Hold a nice flat back.

Stretch your neck out
            n i c e   a n d   l o n g .
This pose makes
        your **tummy** strong!

Bend your elbows,
slowly come down.
Rest your tummy
on the ground.

Keep on breathing, in and out.
Yoga's **hard**, there is no doubt.

Now we stretch
            in **cobra** pose:
lift your shoulders,
            eyes, and nose.

Stretch your chest
            and use your arms.
Show off all your cobra charms.

Toes curl under, hips reach up,
into **downward dog,**

little pup!

Shoulders and back
stretch out so long,
heels press down
and arms are **strong.**

Right foot comes forward
into **lunge** again.
Then both feet forward
for **forward bend.**

Let yourself hang out and
breathe.

Arms are loose,
look at your knees.

Bend your knees
and lift your eyes.
Arms sweep out and up,
breathe in and rise.

Breathe out,
bring hands together
at your chest.
Let's go again...

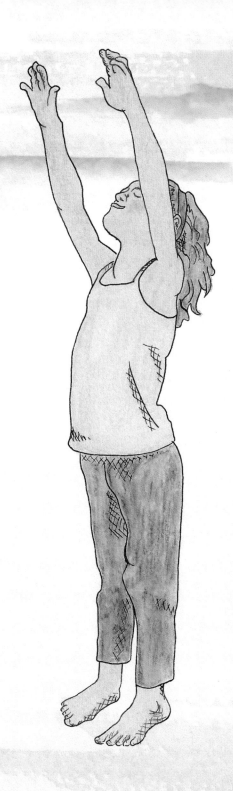

...and do the left.

Stand up tall, chest out—look proud.
Reach your head up toward a cloud.
This is mountain, strong and sure,
rooted in the earth so pure.

Breathe in, reach up, breathe out, dive down.
In forward bend reach toward the ground.
Still keep your legs straight and strong.
Your neck is loose and arms are long.

Monkey is a funny pose:
put hands on shins and lift your nose.
After you take a big breath in,
relax back into forward bend.

In lunge, your left foot reaches back.
Put both hands down to stay on track.
Back leg is straight, front knee over toes.
This is a very powerful pose!

To make a plank, put both feet back.
Keep breathing! Hold a nice flat back.
Stretch your neck out nice and long.
This pose makes your tummy strong!

Bend your elbows, slowly come down.
Rest your tummy on the ground.
Keep on breathing, in and out.
Yoga's hard, there is no doubt.

Now we stretch in cobra pose:
lift your shoulders, eyes, and nose.
Stretch your chest and use your arms.
Show off all your cobra charms.

Toes curl under, hips reach up,
into downward dog, little pup!
Shoulders and back stretch out so long,
heels press down and arms are strong.

Left foot comes forward into lunge again.
Then both feet forward for forward bend.
Let yourself hang out and breathe.
Arms are loose, look at your knees.

Bend your knees
and lift your eyes.
Arms sweep out and up,
breathe in and rise.

Breathe out,
bring hands together
at your chest.

That's the end.
Namaste.
Now let's rest.

Karen Thygerson is a mother, fitness instructor, and yoga enthusiast. She graduated from Pacific Lutheran University with a BA in Psychology and minors in English Literature and Art. After teaching dance and aerobics all her life, she began teaching yoga to her daughter's kindergarten class, and continues to enjoy a weekly practice with her daughter's class. When she's not busy volunteering at her kids' schools, Karen enjoys playing her ukulele, tap dancing, and experimenting with new ways to sneak vegetables into family dinners. Karen lives in San Diego with her husband and their two children.

Thank you to everyone who encouraged and supported me throughout this project and helped make this book possible, especially: Alli Arnold for your guidance, encouragement, and support. Amy Bockelman and Lisa Sparrell for wordsmithing with me and providing invaluable artistic and stylistic feedback. Tavo Adame for sharing your wealth of knowledge about book design. Kristen Hansen Steele for brainstorming artistic methods that led me to my final product. Angela Mietzke for continually championing me and my creative process. Kathleen Gregory for inspiring me to make yoga accessible to kids. Erin Leavitt, Sonia Gomez-Neri, Mayra Onuchic, and all your students for allowing me to come into your classrooms and teach yoga, and igniting the spark that became this book. Keith Thygerson, my husband, friend, and partner, for standing by me and pushing me to accomplish more than I could alone. Jonah Thygerson for inspiring me to be a positive force. And of course my amazing daughter, Lyla, for teaching me to bubble paint, doing art experiments with me, and providing helpful artistic critique and inspiration throughout my process.

Glossary

Yoga:

To unite. Exercise to unite your body and spirit, your breath and movement, your self with the universe.

Namaste:

The light in me recognizes the light in you. I have a Divine spark and so do you. Thank you for being you and for being here.

Sun Salutation:

A time-tested sequence of Yoga poses (with many variations) designed to awaken your body and energize your spirit.

Made in the USA
Lexington, KY
28 April 2014